SCHOLASTIC

Fun Flaps
Word Families

Immacula A. Rhodes

NEW YORK • TORONTO • LONDON • AUCKLAND • SYDNEY
MEXICO CITY • NEW DELHI • HONG KONG • BUENOS AIRES

Teaching *Resources*

Cover design by Maria Lilja
Interior design by Kathy Massaro

ISBN: 978-0-545-28078-5

1 2 3 4 5 6 7 8 9 10   40   18 17 16 15 14 13 12 11

Contents

Word Family Fun Flaps

Short Vowel Word Families

Long Vowel Word Families

Variant Vowel Word Families

Diphthong Word Families

R-Controlled Vowel Word Families

Introduction

Welcome to *Fun Flaps: Word Families*, a hands-on way to help children practice essential reading skills. This book includes 32 reproducible fun flaps that feature the same interactive format that children know and love. Fun flaps are ideal for learning centers or for use during transition times—in the morning, before or after lunch, at the end of the day, or for practice at home.

Each fun flap features related word families. Children choose a picture and name it, then lift the flap to reveal the word and additional words that belong to the same word family. You'll also find additional reproducible pages to make using the fun flaps even easier:

※ step-by-step directions for folding the fun flaps (page 6)

※ a checklist to help children keep track of the fun flaps they've done (page 7)

※ self-checking quizzes (pages 8–15)

※ a fun flap template for children to make their own fun flaps (page 48)

The engaging format and illustrations encourage children to review skills again and again. Mastering word families has never been so much fun!

How to Use This Book

There are many ways these fun flaps can be used in the classroom and at home. Here are some teaching tips to get started.

※ Make copies of the fun flaps, store them in labeled hanging files, and place in a learning center. After demonstrating how to fold the fun flaps, post the folding directions nearby. (Many children already know how to fold these, but the directions will guide them if questions arise.)

※ Have children decorate individualized pocket folders to use for storing their fun flaps, checklists, and quizzes. Explain how to use the checklist to keep track of which fun flaps children have used and to record their quiz scores.

※ Brainstorm with children a list of ways that they might support a productive environment in the classroom while using the fun flaps—for example, speaking in low voices when reading and answering the questions.

Introduce a new fun flap each week. Write the number and title of the fun flap on a sheet of art paper. Then list words that belong to the word families featured on the fun flap. Draw or glue on pictures to go with the words. Invite children to read each word and point out its corresponding picture.

After working with each fun flap, ask children to cut out the self-checking quiz and fold back the right side to hide the answers. Have them complete the quiz and check their work. Then show children how to record their quiz scores as on the checklist.

Using the Fun Flaps

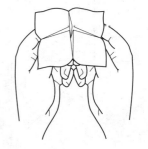

1 Partner A holds the fun flap in a closed position, so that the points touch. Partner A asks Partner B to choose a picture on a flap.

2 Partner B selects one of the four pictures.

3 Partner A opens and closes the fun flap the number of times shown above the selected picture, ending with the fun flap in an open position. Partner A holds the fun flap so Partner B can view the four pictures with word family endings.

4 Partner B chooses a picture and names it. Partner A lifts the flap to reveal the word and reads aloud the other words beneath the flap.

5 Partners can switch roles at any point. Practice continues until both partners have taken several turns and are familiar with the word family words on the fun flap.

Fun Flap Folding Directions

1 Trim off the top part of the fun flap page.

2 Place the fun flap on a flat surface with the blank side facing up.

3 Fold back the four corners along the solid lines so that they touch in the center of the square.

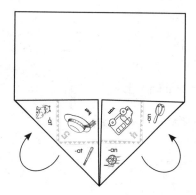

4 Turn over the fun flap. Fold back the corners again so that they touch the center of the square.

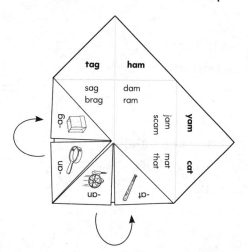

5 Fold the fun flap in half.

6 Place your right thumb and index finger in the right side.

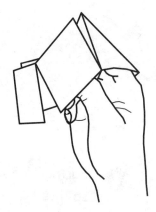

7 Place your left thumb and index finger in the left side.

8 Open and close the fun flap by moving your fingers.

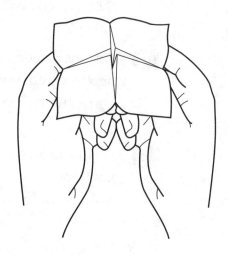

Fun Flaps: Word Families © 2011 by Immacula A. Rhodes, Scholastic Teaching Resources

Name _____

Mark an X under "Fun Flap Practice" after you have practiced with the fun flap.

Mark an X under "Quiz" after you have taken the quiz.

Record your quiz score (how many correct out of 8).

		Fun Flap	Fun Flap Practice	Quiz	Score
Short Vowel Word Families	1	-ag, -am, -an, -at			
	2	-ab, -ack, -ad, -ap			
	3	-amp, -and, -ash, -atch			
	4	-ed, -ell, -en, -et			
	5	-eck, -ell, -ess, -est			
	6	-ig, -in, -ip, -it			
	7	-id, -ig, -in, -ip			
	8	-ick, -ill, -ing, -ink			
	9	-ick, -ill, -ing, -itch			
	10	-ob, -ock, -og, -op			
	11	-ock, -og, -op, -ot			
	12	-ub, -ud, -ug, -un			
	13	-uck, -ug, -um, -ut			
	14	-ump, -unch, -unk, -ust			
Long Vowel Word Families	15	-ake, -ale, -ame, -ate			
	16	-ace, -age, -ane, -ape			
	17	-ake, -ale, -ave, -aze			
	18	-ail, -ain, -ay			
	19	-ea, -each, -eam, -eat			
	20	-eal, -ean, -ee, -eet			
	21	-eed, -eek, -eel, -eep			
	22	-ice, -ide, -ine, -ive			
	23	-ile, -ime, -ipe, -ite			
	24	-ie, -ight, -y			
	25	-oke, -ole, -one, -ose			
	26	-oat, -oe, -old, -ow			
Variant Vowel Word Families	27	-all, -aw, -awn, -ew			
	28	-ook, -ool, -oom, -oot			
Diphthong Word Families	29	-oil, -ow, -own, -oy			
	30	-ouch, -ound, -ouse, -out			
R-Controlled Vowel Word Families	31	-air, -ar, -ark, -art			
	32	-ire, -irt, -ore, -orn			

1

Name _____ Date _____

Write each word. Use the word families in the box to help you.

| -ag -am -an -at |

1. _____   1. fan

2. _____   2. bag

3. _____   3. cat

4. _____   4. yam

5. _____   5. tag

6. _____   6. ham

7. _____   7. van

8. _____   8. bat

Fold back here.

2

Name _____ Date _____

Write each word. Use the word families in the box to help you.

| -ab -ack -ad -ap |

1. _____   1. mad

2. _____   2. back

3. _____   3. crab

4. _____   4. cap

5. _____   5. tack

6. _____   6. lab

7. _____   7. map

8. _____   8. sad

Fold back here.

3

Name _____ Date _____

Write each word. Use the word families in the box to help you.

| -amp -and -ash -atch |

1. _____   1. hand

2. _____   2. trash

3. _____   3. patch

4. _____   4. cash

5. _____   5. match

6. _____   6. lamp

7. _____   7. sand

8. _____   8. stamp

Fold back here.

4

Name _____ Date _____

Write each word. Use the word families in the box to help you.

| -ed -ell -en -et |

1. _____   1. ten

2. _____   2. net

3. _____   3. shell

4. _____   4. bed

5. _____   5. hen

6. _____   6. jet

7. _____   7. shed

8. _____   8. bell

Fold back here.

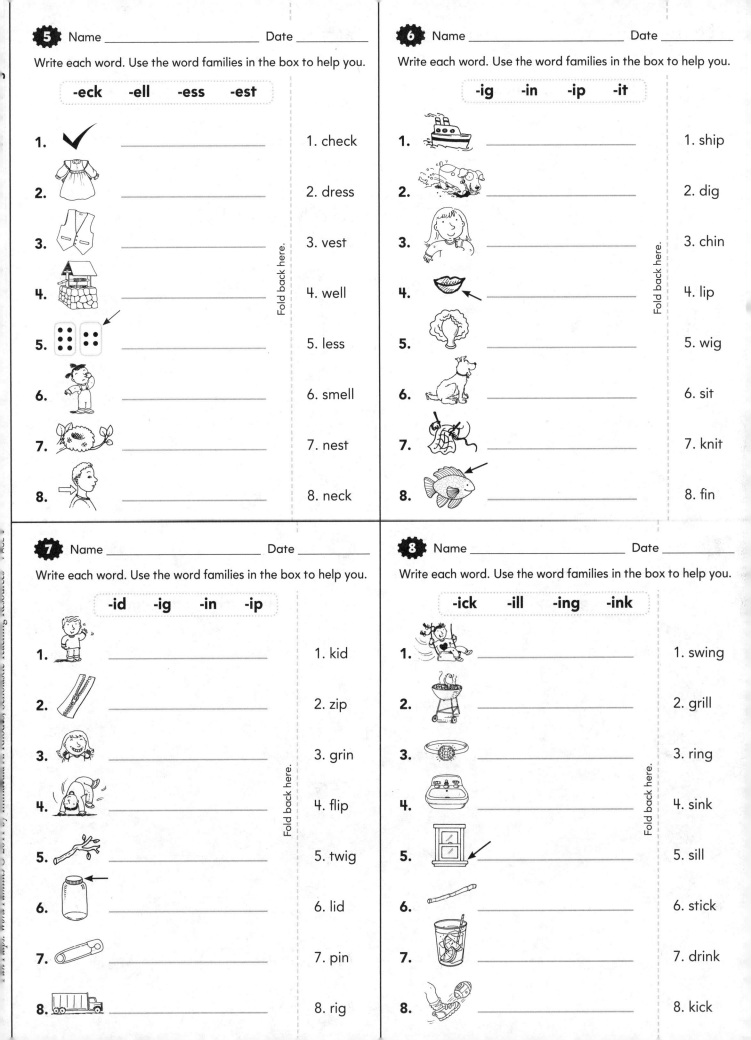

5 Name _____ Date _____

Write each word. Use the word families in the box to help you.

| -eck | -ell | -ess | -est |

1. ✔ _____   1. check
2. _____   2. dress
3. _____   3. vest
4. _____   4. well
5. _____   5. less
6. _____   6. smell
7. _____   7. nest
8. _____   8. neck

Fold back here.

6 Name _____ Date _____

Write each word. Use the word families in the box to help you.

| -ig | -in | -ip | -it |

1. _____   1. ship
2. _____   2. dig
3. _____   3. chin
4. _____   4. lip
5. _____   5. wig
6. _____   6. sit
7. _____   7. knit
8. _____   8. fin

Fold back here.

7 Name _____ Date _____

Write each word. Use the word families in the box to help you.

| -id | -ig | -in | -ip |

1. _____   1. kid
2. _____   2. zip
3. _____   3. grin
4. _____   4. flip
5. _____   5. twig
6. _____   6. lid
7. _____   7. pin
8. _____   8. rig

Fold back here.

8 Name _____ Date _____

Write each word. Use the word families in the box to help you.

| -ick | -ill | -ing | -ink |

1. _____   1. swing
2. _____   2. grill
3. _____   3. ring
4. _____   4. sink
5. _____   5. sill
6. _____   6. stick
7. _____   7. drink
8. _____   8. kick

Fold back here.

Name _____ Date _____

Write each word. Use the word families in the box to help you.

| -ick | -ill | -ing | -itch |

1. _____   1. witch

2. _____   2. chick

3. _____   3. pill

4. _____   4. sing

5. _____   5. switch

6. _____   6. brick

7. _____   7. chill

8. _____   8. wing

Fold back here.

Name _____ Date _____

Write each word. Use the word families in the box to help you.

| -ob | -ock | -og | -op |

1. _____   1. mop

2. _____   2. sock

3. _____   3. sob

4. _____   4. clock

5. _____   5. knob

6. _____   6. log

7. _____   7. stop

8. _____   8. frog

Fold back here.

Name _____ Date _____

Write each word. Use the word families in the box to help you.

| -ock | -og | -op | -ot |

1. _____   1. block

2. _____   2. jog

3. _____   3. cot

4. _____   4. top

5. _____   5. knot

6. _____   6. cop

7. _____   7. lock

8. _____   8. hog

Fold back here.

Name _____ Date _____

Write each word. Use the word families in the box to help you.

| -ub | -uck | -ud | -un |

1. _____   1. sun

2. _____   2. bud

3. _____   3. cub

4. _____   4. mug

5. _____   5. tub

6. _____   6. bun

7. _____   7. spud

8. _____   8. rug

Fold back here.

Name _____ Date _____

Write each word. Use the word families in the box to help you.

-uck -ug -um -ut

1. 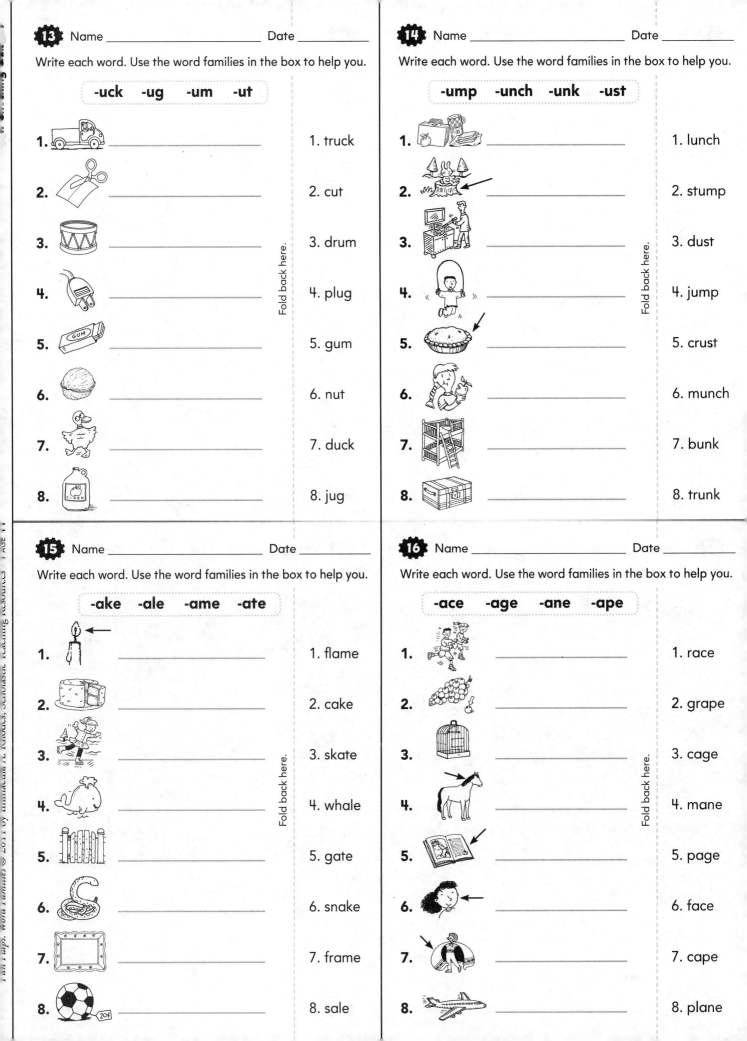 _____
2. _____
3. _____
4. _____
5. _____
6. _____
7. _____
8. _____

Fold back here.

1. truck
2. cut
3. drum
4. plug
5. gum
6. nut
7. duck
8. jug

---

14 Name _____ Date _____

Write each word. Use the word families in the box to help you.

-ump -unch -unk -ust

1. _____
2. _____
3. _____
4. _____
5. _____
6. _____
7. _____
8. _____

Fold back here.

1. lunch
2. stump
3. dust
4. jump
5. crust
6. munch
7. bunk
8. trunk

---

15 Name _____ Date _____

Write each word. Use the word families in the box to help you.

-ake -ale -ame -ate

1. _____
2. _____
3. _____
4. _____
5. _____
6. _____
7. _____
8. _____

Fold back here.

1. flame
2. cake
3. skate
4. whale
5. gate
6. snake
7. frame
8. sale

---

16 Name _____ Date _____

Write each word. Use the word families in the box to help you.

-ace -age -ane -ape

1. _____
2. _____
3. _____
4. _____
5. _____
6. _____
7. _____
8. _____

Fold back here.

1. race
2. grape
3. cage
4. mane
5. page
6. face
7. cape
8. plane

17 Name _____ Date _____

Write each word. Use the word families in the box to help you.

-ake   -ale   -ave   -aze

1. _____   1. scale
2. _____   2. blaze
3. _____   3. male
4. _____   4. rake
5. _____   5. wave
6. _____   6. flake
7. _____   7. cave
8. _____   8. maze

Fold back here.

18 Name _____ Date _____

Write each word. Use the word families in the box to help you.

-ail   -ain   -ay

1. _____   1. snail
2. _____   2. train
3. _____   3. pail
4. _____   4. hay
5. _____   5. tray
6. _____   6. trail
7. _____   7. chain
8. _____   8. nail

Fold back here.

19 Name _____ Date _____

Write each word. Use the word families in the box to help you.

-ea   -each   -eam   -eat

1. _____   1. dream
2. _____   2. peach
3. _____   3. pea
4. _____   4. steam
5. _____   5. reach
6. _____   6. meat
7. _____   7. heat
8. _____   8. sea

Fold back here.

20 Name _____ Date _____

Write each word. Use the word families in the box to help you.

-eal   -ean   -ee   -eet

1. _____   1. meal
2. _____   2. bean
3. _____   3. feet
4. _____   4. bee
5. _____   5. lean
6. _____   6. seal
7. _____   7. tree
8. _____   8. street

Fold back here.

21 Name _____ Date _____

Write each word. Use the word families in the box to help you.

| -eed -eek -eel -eep |

1. _____
2. _____
3. _____
4. _____
5. _____
6. _____
7. _____
8. _____

Fold back here.

1. cheek
2. jeep
3. speed
4. sheep
5. wheel
6. seed
7. peel
8. peek

---

22 Name _____ Date _____

Write each word. Use the word families in the box to help you.

| -ice -ide -ine -ive |

1. _____
2. _____
3. _____
4. _____
5. _____
6. _____
7. _____
8. _____

Fold back here.

1. ice
2. hive
3. nine
4. slide
5. dive
6. bride
7. mice
8. vine

---

23 Name _____ Date _____

Write each word. Use the word families in the box to help you.

| -ile -ime -ipe -ite |

1. _____
2. _____
3. _____
4. _____
5. _____
6. _____
7. _____
8. _____

Fold back here.

1. write
2. smile
3. dime
4. pipe
5. file
6. stripe
7. kite
8. time

---

24 Name _____ Date _____

Write each word. Use the word families in the box to help you.

| -ie -ight -y |

1. _____
2. _____
3. _____
4. _____
5. _____
6. _____
7. _____
8. _____

Fold back here.

1. knight
2. tie
3. fright
4. light
5. fly
6. right
7. dry
8. pie

25

Name _____ Date _____

Write each word. Use the word families in the box to help you.

-oke   **-ole**   **-one**   **-ose**

1. 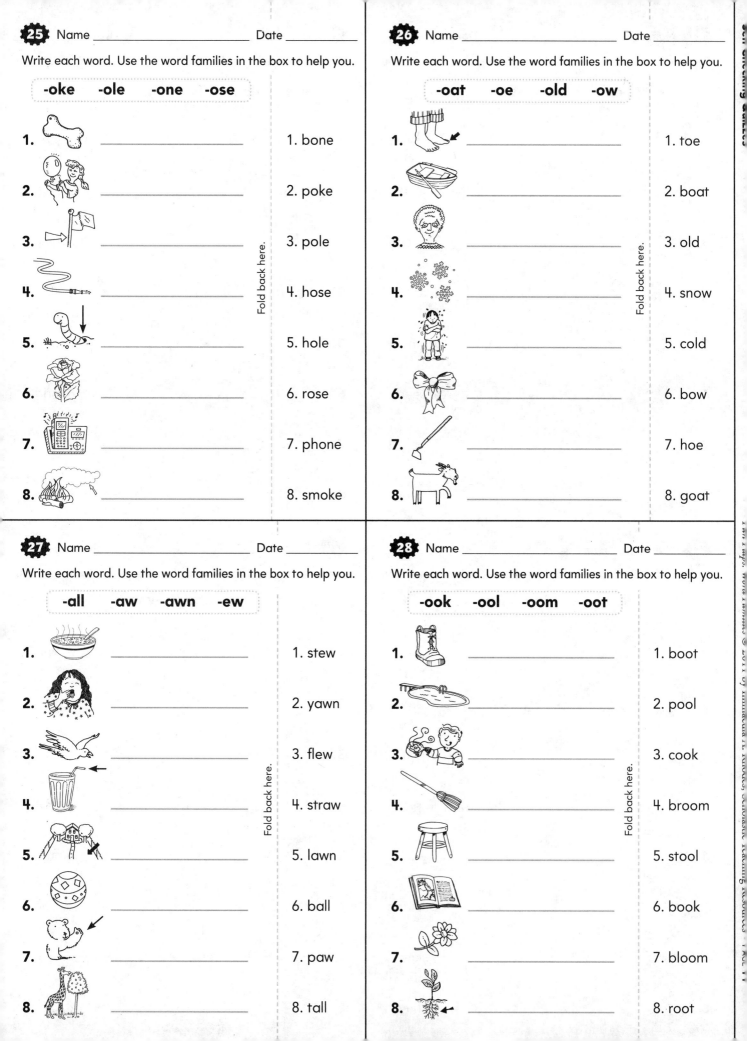 _____

2. _____

3. _____

4. _____

5. _____

6. _____

7. _____

8. _____

Fold back here.

1. bone

2. poke

3. pole

4. hose

5. hole

6. rose

7. phone

8. smoke

26

Name _____ Date _____

Write each word. Use the word families in the box to help you.

-oat   **-oe**   **-old**   **-ow**

1. _____

2. _____

3. _____

4. _____

5. _____

6. _____

7. _____

8. _____

Fold back here.

1. toe

2. boat

3. old

4. snow

5. cold

6. bow

7. hoe

8. goat

27

Name _____ Date _____

Write each word. Use the word families in the box to help you.

-all   **-aw**   **-awn**   **-ew**

1. _____

2. _____

3. _____

4. _____

5. _____

6. _____

7. _____

8. _____

Fold back here.

1. stew

2. yawn

3. flew

4. straw

5. lawn

6. ball

7. paw

8. tall

28

Name _____ Date _____

Write each word. Use the word families in the box to help you.

-ook   **-ool**   **-oom**   **-oot**

1. _____

2. _____

3. _____

4. _____

5. _____

6. _____

7. _____

8. _____

Fold back here.

1. boot

2. pool

3. cook

4. broom

5. stool

6. book

7. bloom

8. root

Name _____ Date _____

Write each word. Use the word families in the box to help you.

| **-oil   -ow   -own   -oy** |

1. _____   1. soil
2. _____   2. plow
3. _____   3. toy
4. _____   4. crown
5. _____   5. boy
6. _____   6. boil
7. _____   7. cow
8. _____   8. clown

Fold back here.

Name _____ Date _____

Write each word. Use the word families in the box to help you.

| **-ouch   -ound   -ouse   -out** |

1. _____   1. mound
2. _____   2. house
3. _____   3. couch
4. _____   4. spout
5. _____   5. grouch
6. _____   6. hound
7. _____   7. mouse
8. _____   8. shout

Fold back here.

Name _____ Date _____

Write each word. Use the word families in the box to help you.

| **-air   -ar   -ark   -art** |

1. _____   1. car
2. _____   2. shark
3. _____   3. hair
4. _____   4. dart
5. _____   5. star
6. _____   6. chair
7. _____   7. cart
8. _____   8. park

Fold back here.

Name _____ Date _____

Write each word. Use the word families in the box to help you.

| **-ire   -irt   -ore   -orn** |

1. _____   1. corn
2. _____   2. shirt
3. _____   3. dirt
4. _____   4. snore
5. _____   5. tire
6. _____   6. horn
7. _____   7. shore
8. _____   8. fire

Fold back here.

1 -ag, -am, -an, -at

Name the picture. Add the beginning sound to the word family ending.
Pick your favorite picture to start.

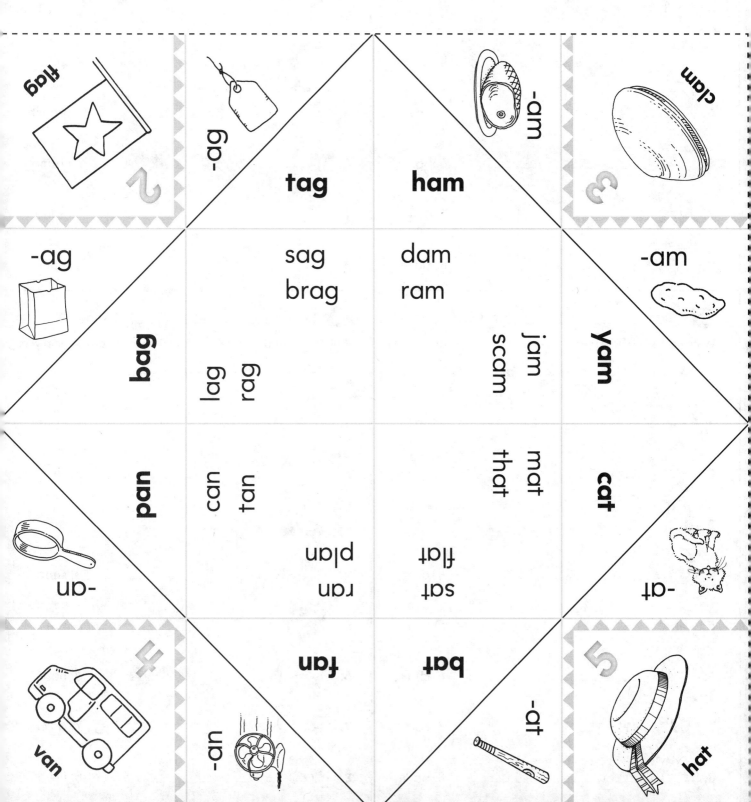

flag

2

-ag

tag

ham

-am

clam

3

-ag

sag
brag

dam
ram

-am

bag

lag rag

jam
scam

yam

pan

can tan

mat
that

cat

-an

plan
ran

sat
flat

-at

fan

bat

4

-an

-at

5

van

hat

2 -ab, -ack, -ad, -ap

Name the picture. Add the beginning sound to the word family ending.
Pick your favorite picture to start.

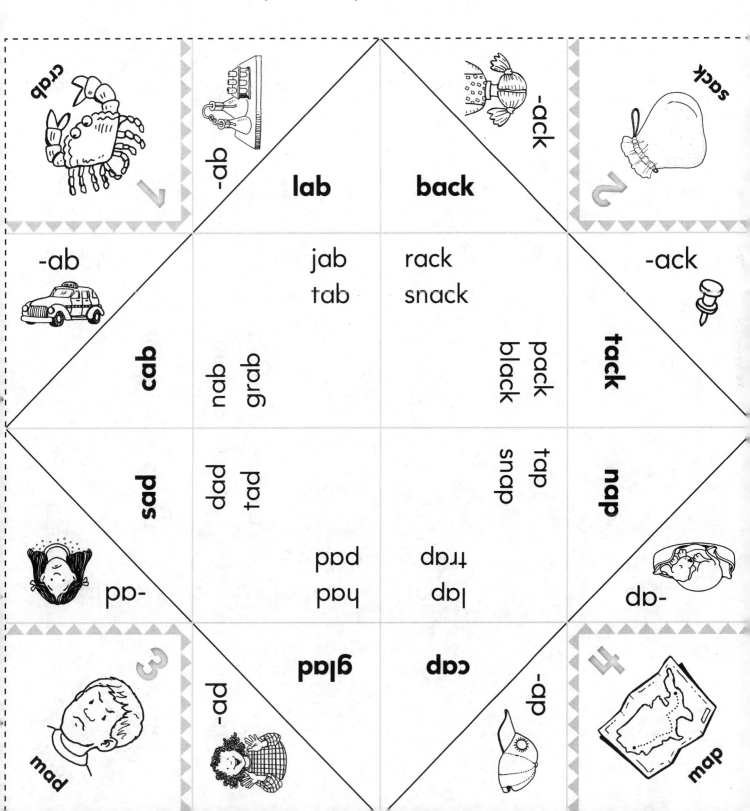

crab

-ab

lab   back

-ack

sack

1

-ab

jab   rack

tab   snack

2

-ack

cab

nab grab

pack
black

tack

sad

dad tad

tap
snap

nap

-ad

pad
had

trap
lap

-ap

glad   cap

3

-ad

4

-ap

map

mad

3 -amp, -and, -ash, -atch

Name the picture. Add the beginning sound to the word family ending.
Pick your favorite picture to start.

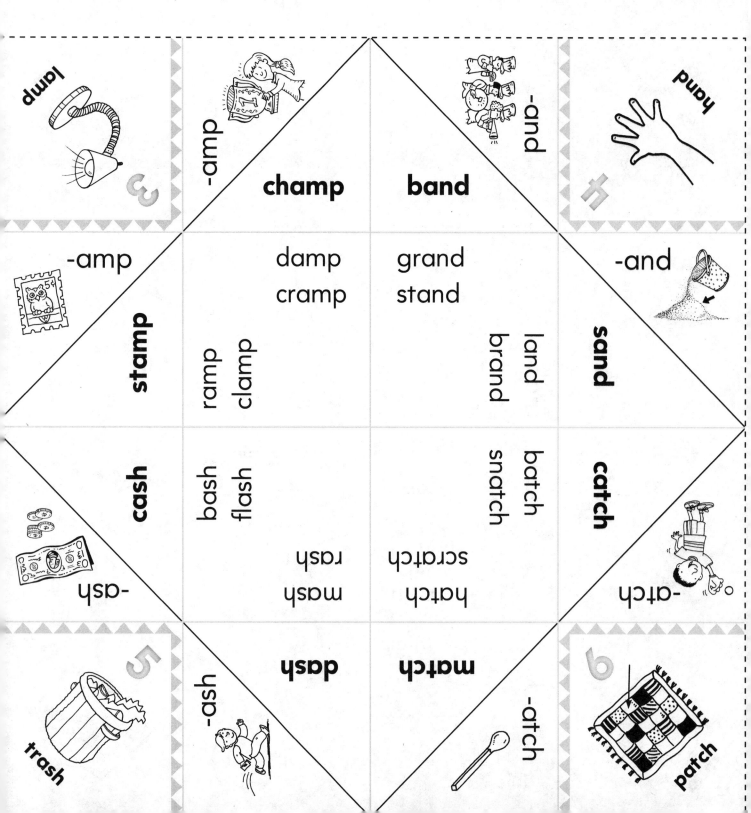

4 -ed, -ell, -en, -et

Name the picture. Add the beginning sound to the word family ending.
Pick your favorite picture to start.

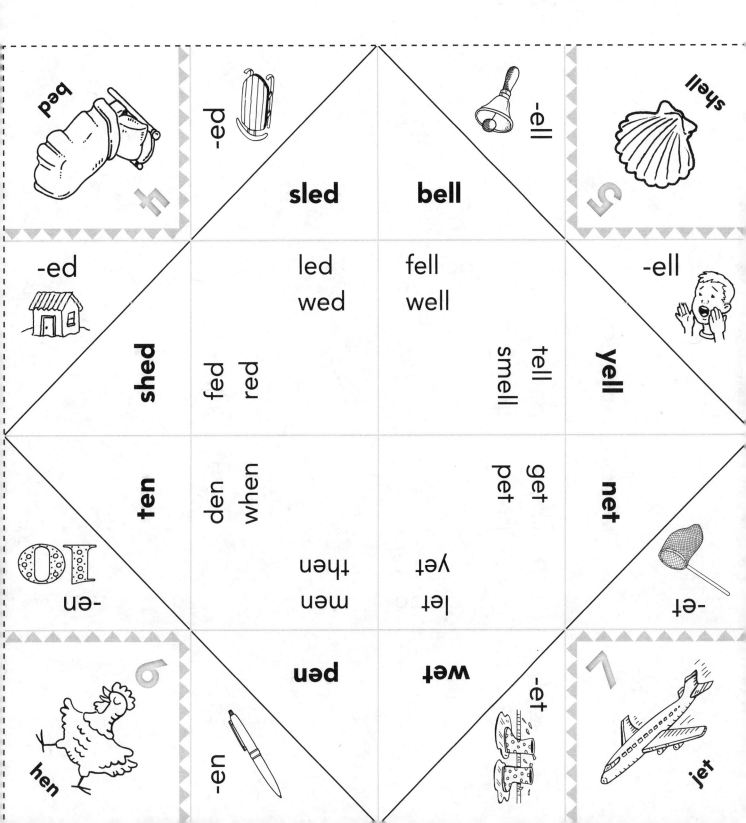

bed

-ed

-ell

shell

sled

bell

-ed

led
wed

fell
well

-ell

shed

fed
red

tell
smell

yell

ten

den   when

get
pet

net

10

-en

then
men

yet
let

wet

pen

-et

hen

-en

-et

7

jet

5 -eck, -ell, -ess, -est

Name the picture. Add the beginning sound to the word family ending.
Pick your favorite picture to start.

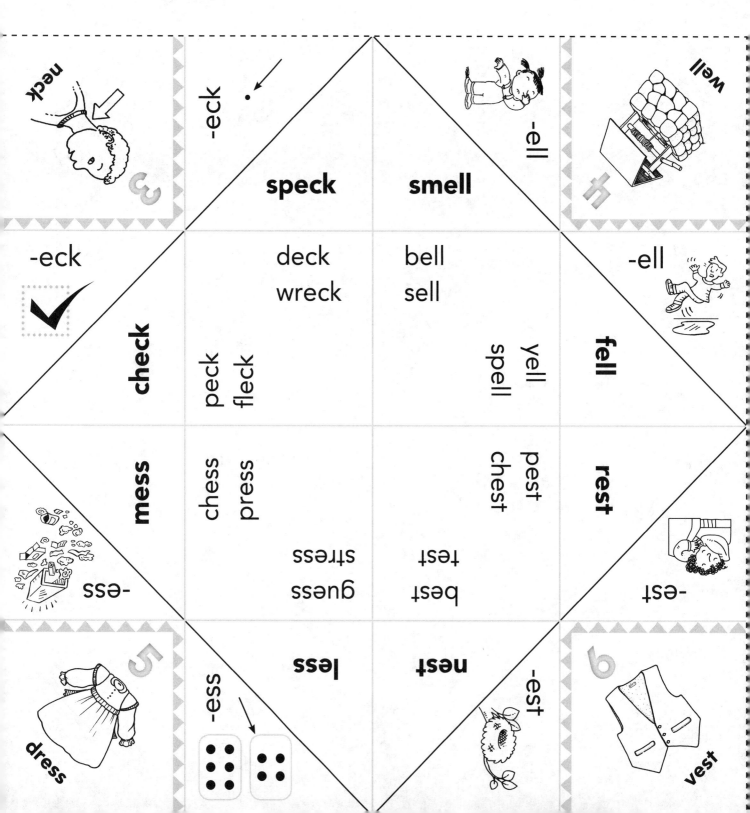

neck
3

-eck

speck

smell

-ell
4

well

-eck

✓

check

deck
wreck

peck
fleck

bell
sell

yell
spell

-ell

fell

mess

chess
press

chest
pest

rest

-ess

stress
guess

best
test

-est

dress
5

-ess

less

nest

-est
6

vest

Skill > Short *i* Word Families

6 -ig, -in, -ip, -it

Name the picture. Add the beginning sound to the word family ending.
Pick your favorite picture to start.

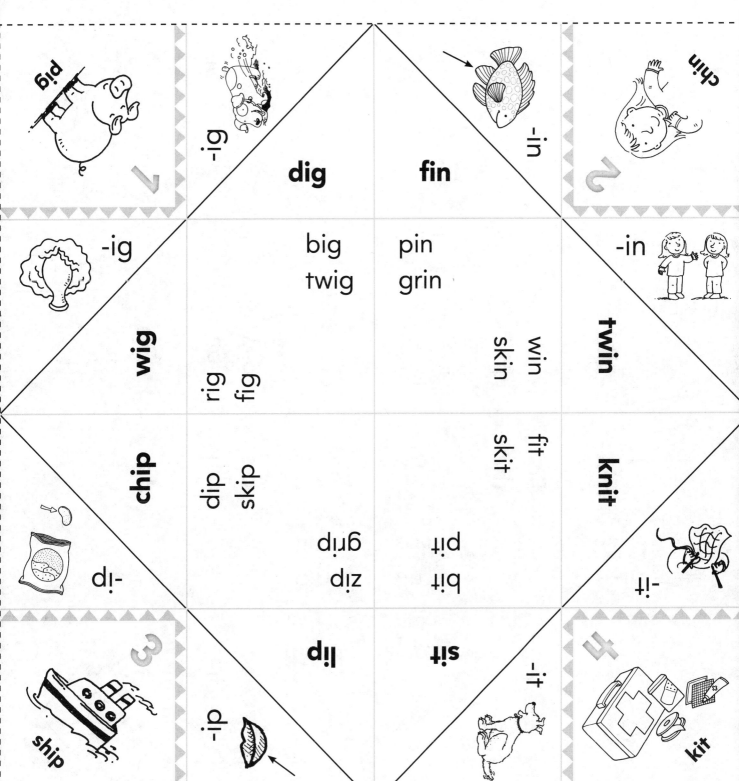

pig

-ig

-in

chin

-ig

dig

fin

-in

wig

big
twig

pin
grin

twin

rig
fig

win
skin

chip

dip
skip

fit
skit

knit

-ip

grip
zip

pit
bit

-it

lip

sit

-ip

-it

ship

kit

7 -id, -ig, -in, -ip

Name the picture. Add the beginning sound to the word family ending.
Pick your favorite picture to start.

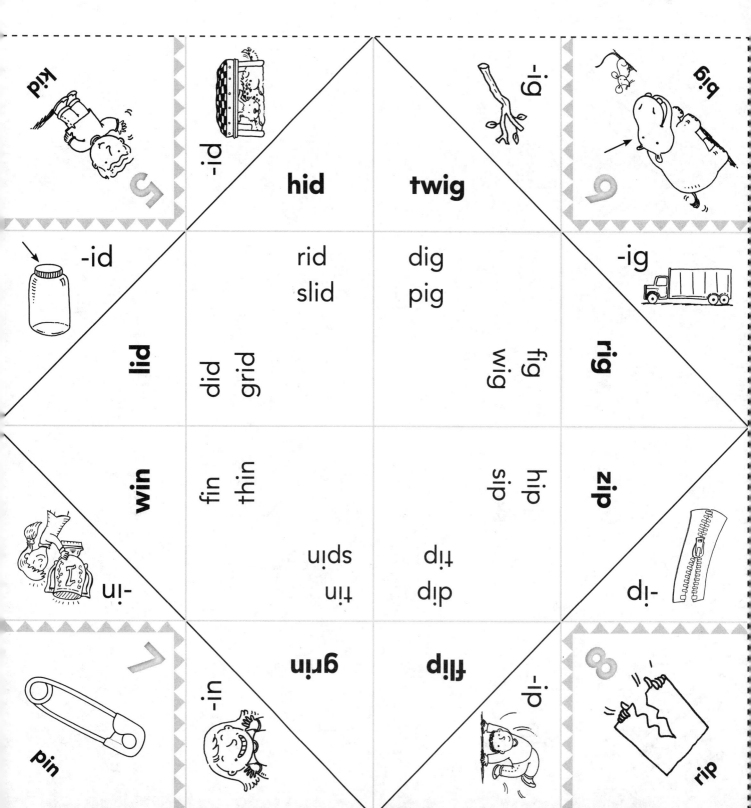

kid 5

-id

-ig

pig 6

hid

twig

-id

rid

slid

dig

pig

-ig

lid

did grid

fig wig

rig

win

fin thin

hip sip

zip

-in

spin fin

tip dip

-ip

pin 7

-in

grin

flip

-ip

rip 8

8 -ick, -ill, -ing, -ink

Name the picture. Add the beginning sound to the word family ending.
Pick your favorite picture to start.

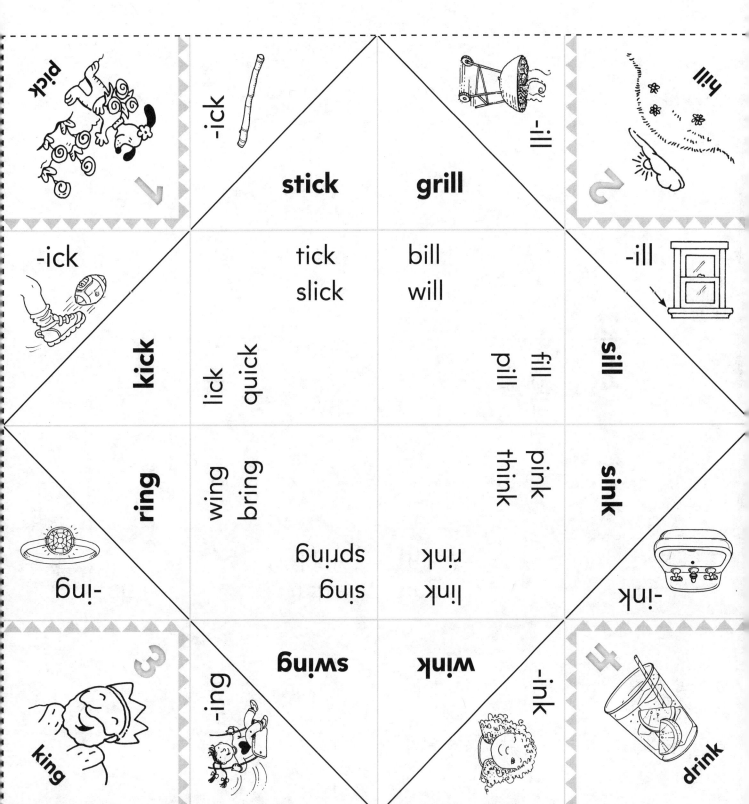

9 -ick, -ill, -ing, -itch

Name the picture. Add the beginning sound to the word family ending.
Pick your favorite picture to start.

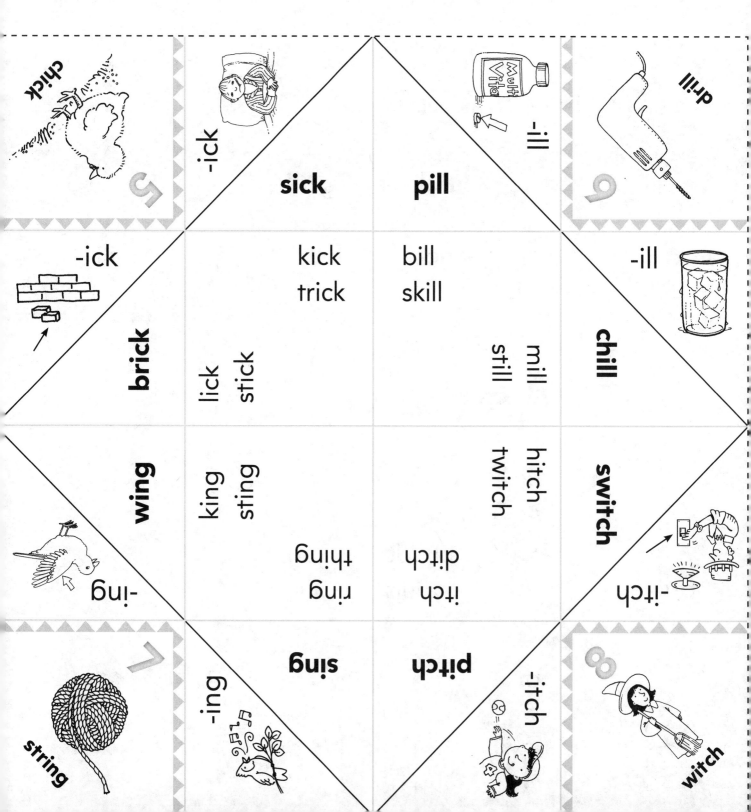

10 -ob, -ock, -og, -op

Name the picture. Add the beginning sound to the word family ending. Pick your favorite picture to start.

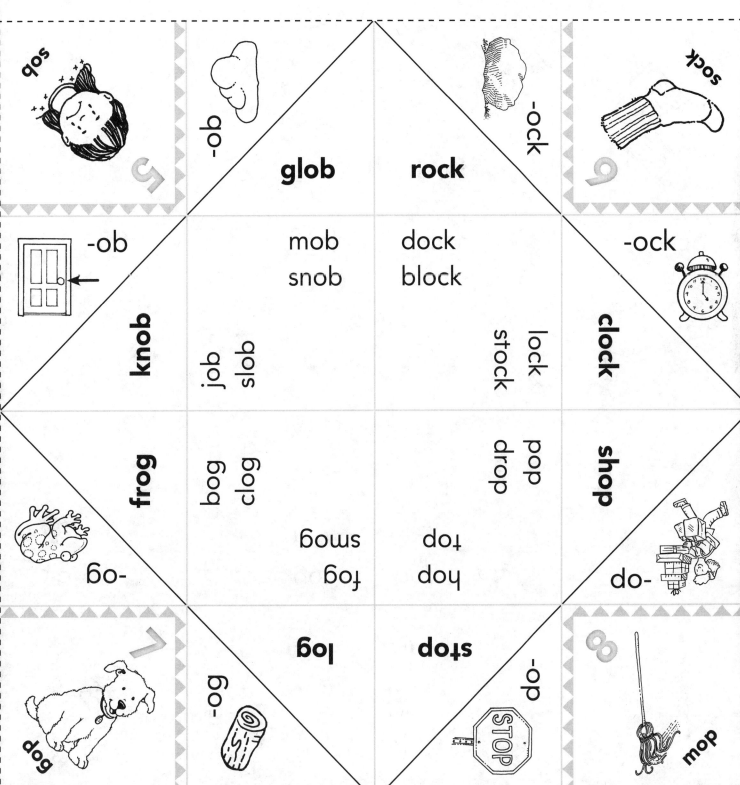

sob

-ob

glob   rock

-ock

sock
5

-ob

mob   dock

snob   block

-ock

clock

knob

job   slob   lock
                    stock

clock

frog

bog   clog   pop
                    drop

shop

fog   smog   top
fog   hop

-op

-og

log   stop

dog

-og

-op

mop
7

8

11 -ock, -og, -op, -ot

Name the picture. Add the beginning sound to the word family ending.
Pick your favorite picture to start.

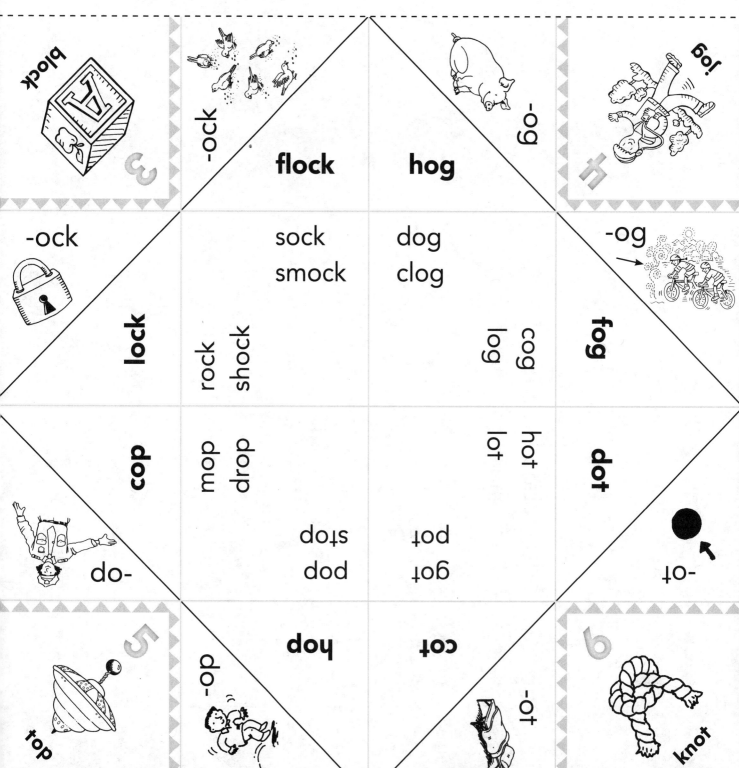

block

3

-ock

flock

hog

-og

4

-ock

sock
smock

dog
clog

-og

lock

rock
shock

cog
log

fog

cop

mop
drop

hot
lot

dot

-op

stop
pop

pot
got

-ot

hop

cot

top

5

-op

knot

6

-ot

12 -ub, -ud, -ug, -un

Name the picture. Add the beginning sound to the word family ending.
Pick your favorite picture to start.

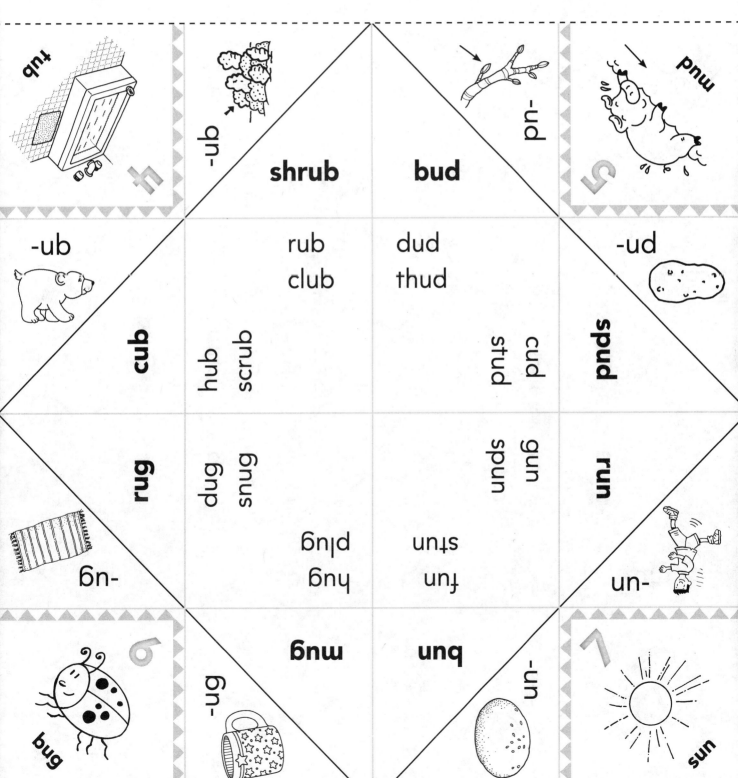

tub

-ub

shrub

bud

-un

mud

5

-ub

cub

rub
club

dud
thud

-ud

spud

hub
scrub

cud
stud

rug

dug
snug

gun
spun

run

-ug

plug
hug

stun
fun

un-

mug

bun

-un

bug

-ug

sun

7

13 -uck, -ug, -um, -ut

Name the picture. Add the beginning sound to the word family ending.
Pick your favorite picture to start.

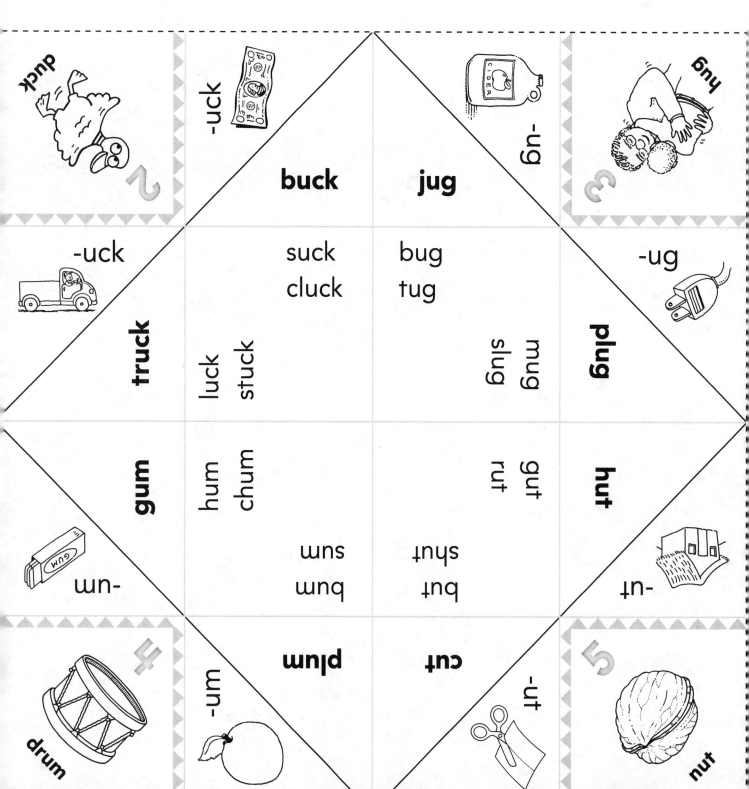

duck

-uck

-ug

hug

-uck

truck

buck

suck
cluck

luck   stuck

jug

bug
tug

mug
slug

plug

-ug

gum

hum   chum

sum
bum

shut
but

gut
rut

hut

-ut

-um

drum

-um

plum

cut

-ut

nut

14 -ump, -unch, -unk, -ust

Name the picture. Add the beginning sound to the word family ending.
Pick your favorite picture to start.

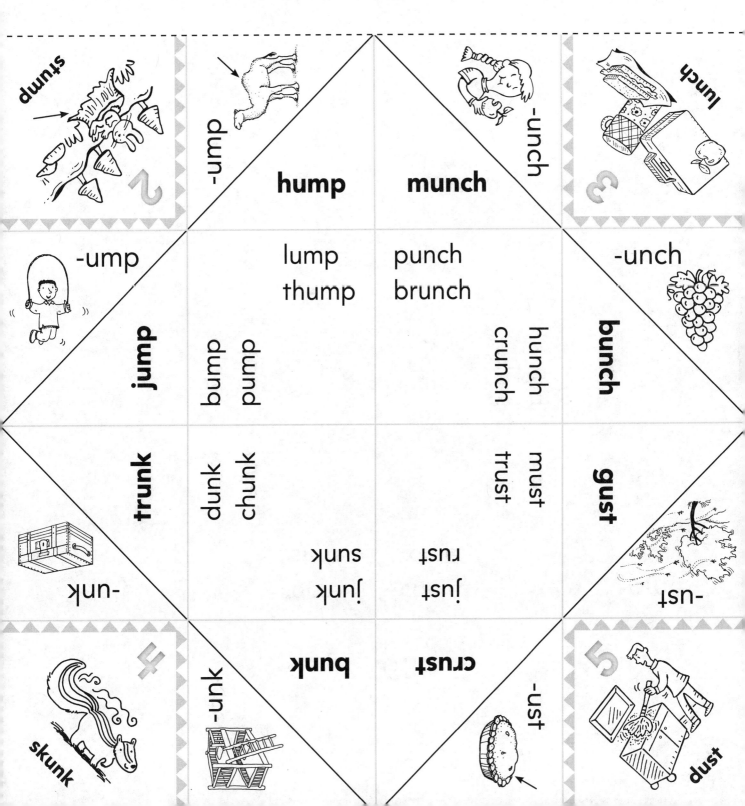

stump

-ump

hump

munch

-unch

lunch

-ump

lump
thump

punch
brunch

-unch

jump

bump
pump

hunch
crunch

bunch

trunk

dunk
chunk

must
trust

gust

-unk

sunk
junk

rust
just

-ust

skunk

-unk

dunk

crust

-ust

dust

15 -ake, -ale, -ame, -ate

Name the picture. Add the beginning sound to the word family ending.
Pick your favorite picture to start.

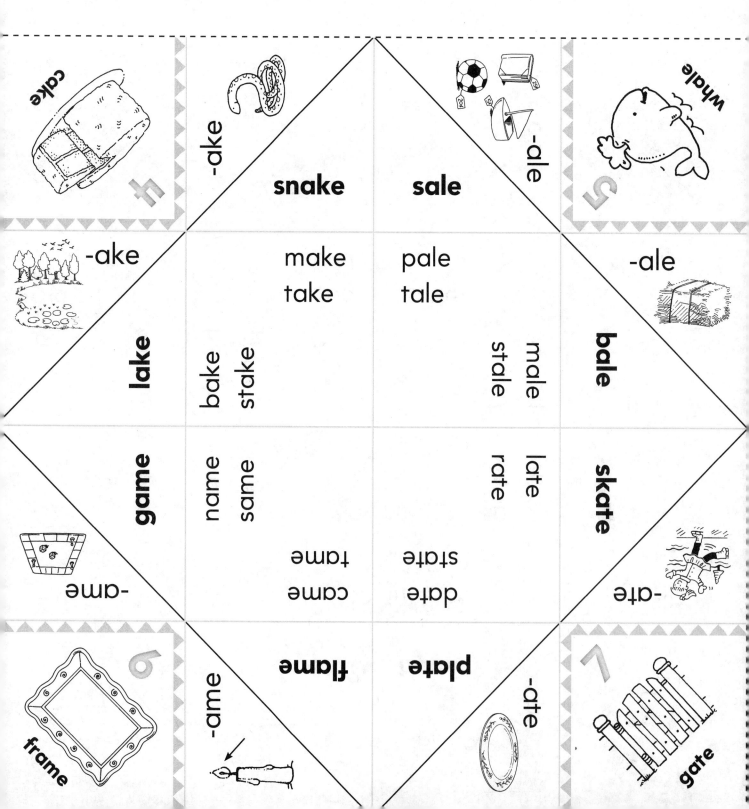

cake

4

-ake

snake

sale

-ale

whale

5

-ake

lake

make
take

pale
tale

male
stale

-ale

bale

game

bake
stake

name
same

state
date

tale
state

late
rate

skate

-ame

frame

6

-ame

flame

plate

-ate

gate

7

-ate

16 -ace, -age, -ane, -ape

Name the picture. Add the beginning sound to the word family ending.
Pick your favorite picture to start.

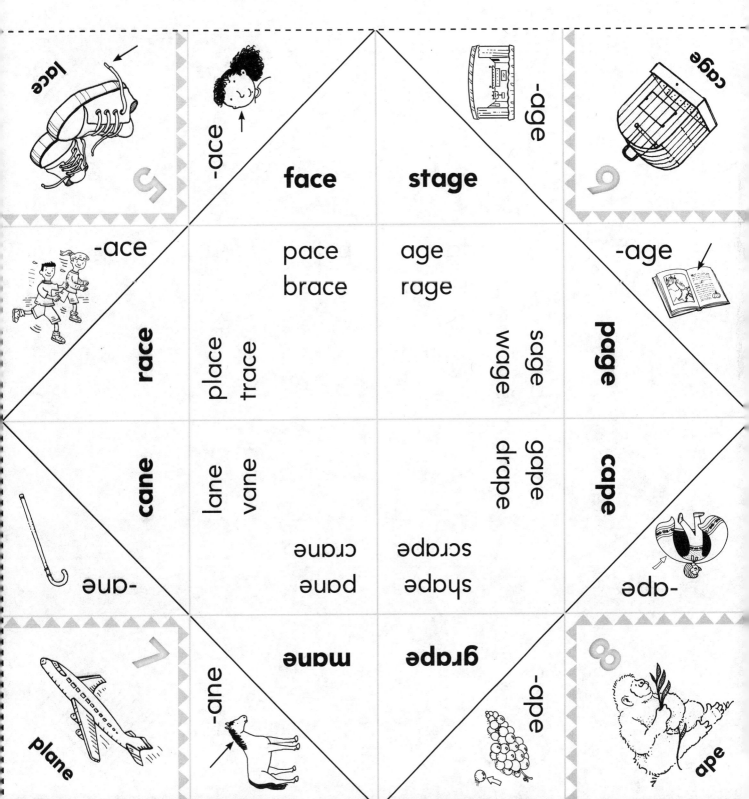

lace

-ace

-age

cage

-ace

-age

page

race

face

stage

pace
brace

age
rage

place
trace

sage
wage

cane

cape

lane
vane

gape
drape

crane
pane

scrape
shape

-ane

-ape

plane

mane

grape

-ape

ape

-ane

17 -ake, -ale, -ave, -aze

Name the picture. Add the beginning sound to the word family ending.
Pick your favorite picture to start.

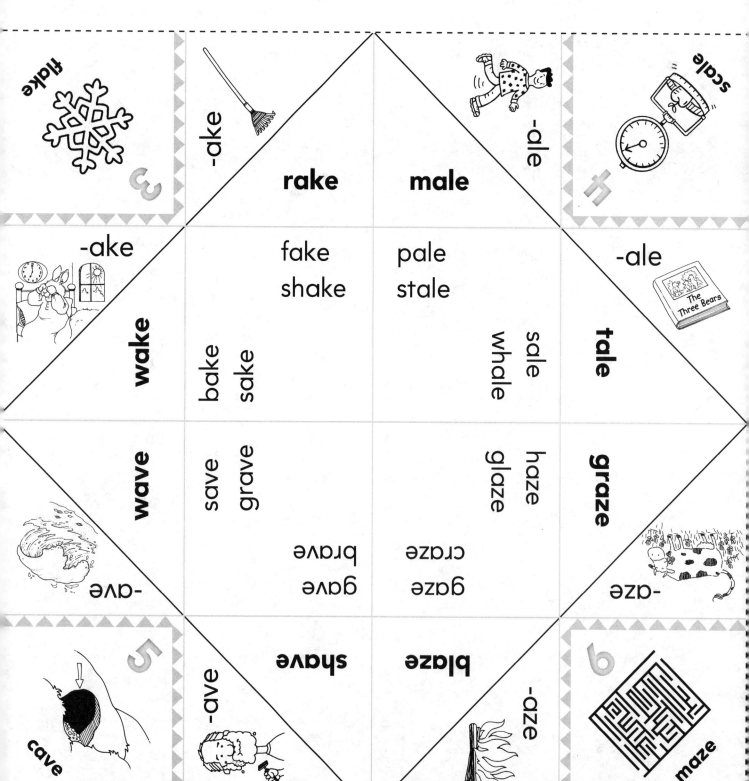

flake

3

-ake

rake   male

-ale

4

scale

-ake

wake

fake
shake

pale
stale

sale
whale

tale

-ale

The Three Bears

bake   sake

save   grave

wave

haze
glaze

graze

brave
gave

craze
gaze

-ave

5

cave

-ave

shave

blaze

-aze

-aze

6

maze

18 -ail, -ain, -ay

Name the picture. Add the beginning sound to the word family ending.
Pick your favorite picture to start.

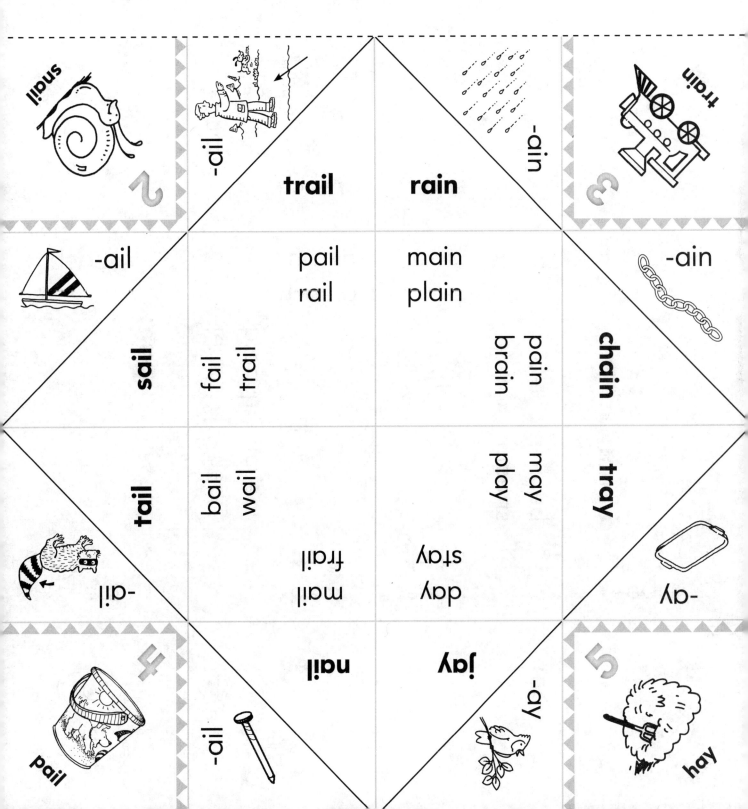

snail

2

-ail

trail   rain

-ain

3

train

-ail

sail

pail
rail

main
plain

-ain

fail trail

pain
brain

chain

tail

bail wail

may
play

tray

-ail

trail
mail

stay
day

-ay

4

nail

jay

5

pail

-ail

-ay

hay

19 -ea, -each, -eam, -eat

Name the picture. Add the beginning sound to the word family ending.
Pick your favorite picture to start.

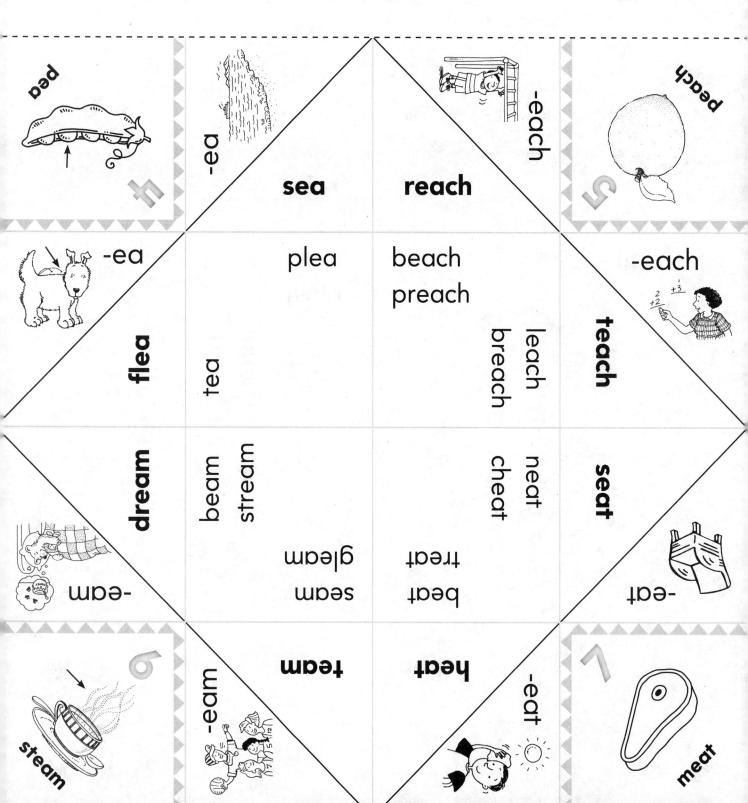

pea

-ea

sea   reach

-each

peach

-ea

flea

plea

tea

beach
preach

leach
breach

teach

-each

dream

beam
stream

neat
cheat

seat

-eam

gleam
seam

beat
treat

-eat

team   heat

-eam

-eat

steam

meat

20 -eal, -ean, -ee, -eet

Name the picture. Add the beginning sound to the word family ending. Pick your favorite picture to start.

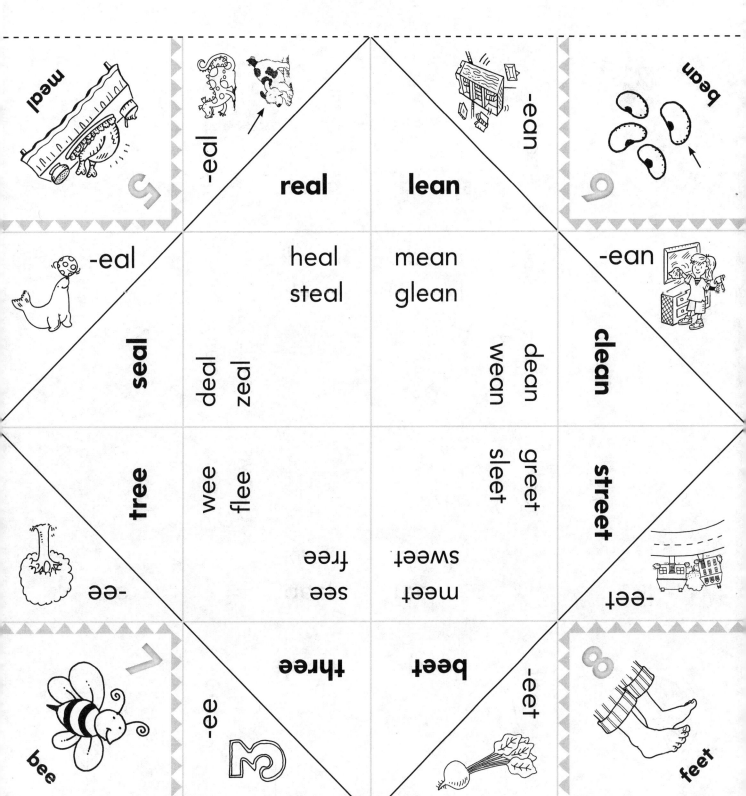

21 -eed, -eek, -eel, -eep

Name the picture. Add the beginning sound to the word family ending.
Pick your favorite picture to start.

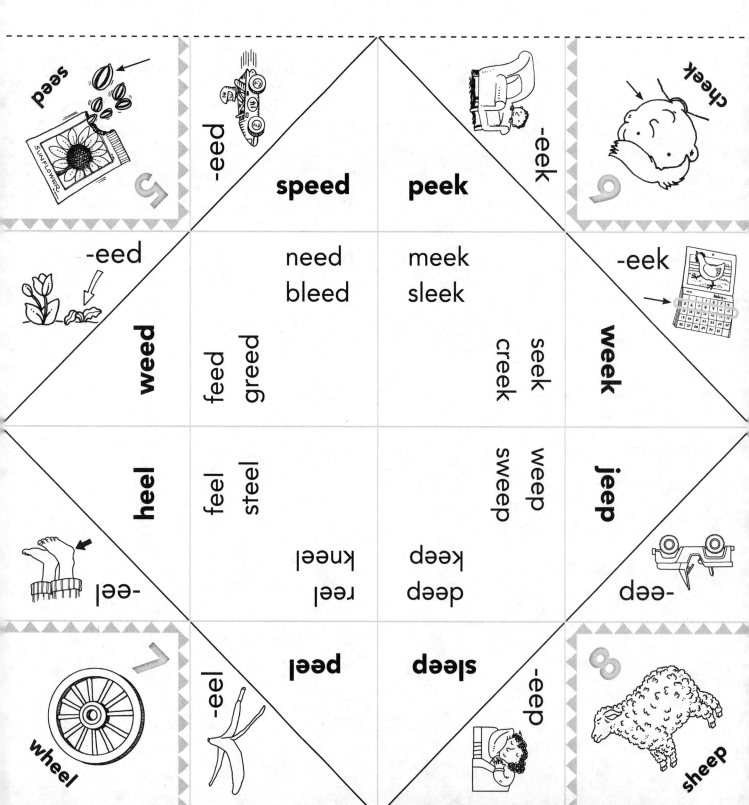

seed

-eed

-eek

cheek

speed

peek

-eed

need
bleed

meek
sleek

-eek

week

weed

feed
greed

seek
creek

heel

feel
steel

weep
sweep

jeep

-eel

kneel
reel

keep
deep

-eep

peel

sleep

-eel

-eep

wheel

sheep

22 -ice, -ide, -ine, -ive

Name the picture. Add the beginning sound to the word family ending.
Pick your favorite picture to start.

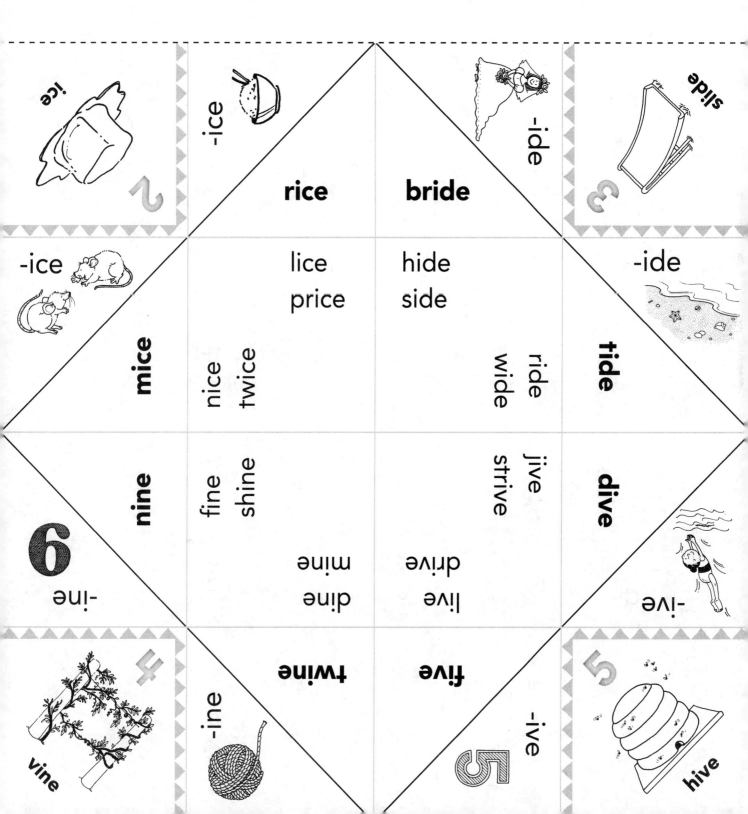

ice

-ice

-ide

slide

rice   **bride**

-ice

-ide

mice

lice   hide
price   side

tide

nice twice   ride wide

nine   dive

fine shine   jive strive

6

-ine

-ive

mine dine   live drive

vine

-ine

twine   five

hive

-ive

5

23 -ile, -ime, -ipe, -ite

Name the picture. Add the beginning sound to the word family ending.
Pick your favorite picture to start.

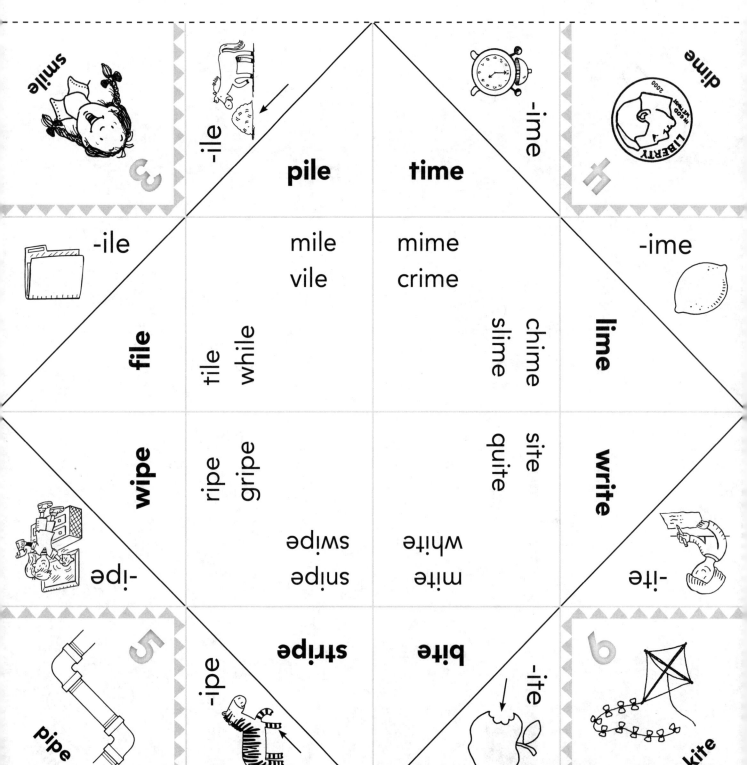

smile

3

-ile

pile

time

-ime

4

dime

-ile

mile
vile

mime
crime

-ime

file

tile while

chime
slime

lime

wipe

ripe gripe

site
quite

write

-ipe-

swipe
snipe

mite
white

-ite-

5

pipe

-ipe

stripe

bite

-ite

6

kite

24 -ie, -ight, -y

Name the picture. Add the beginning sound to the word family ending.
Pick your favorite picture to start.

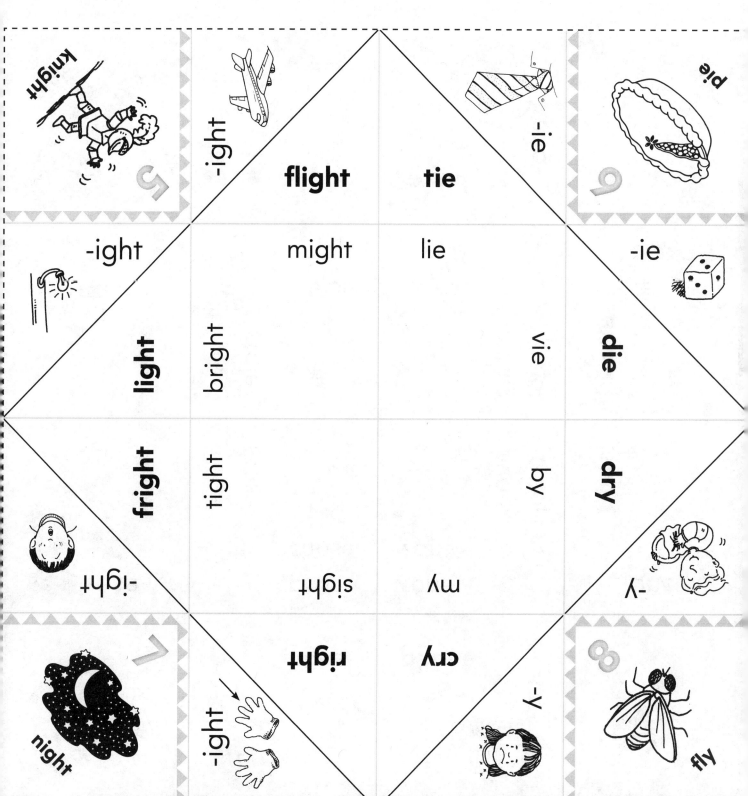

25 -oke, -ole, -one, -ose

Name the picture. Add the beginning sound to the word family ending.
Pick your favorite picture to start.

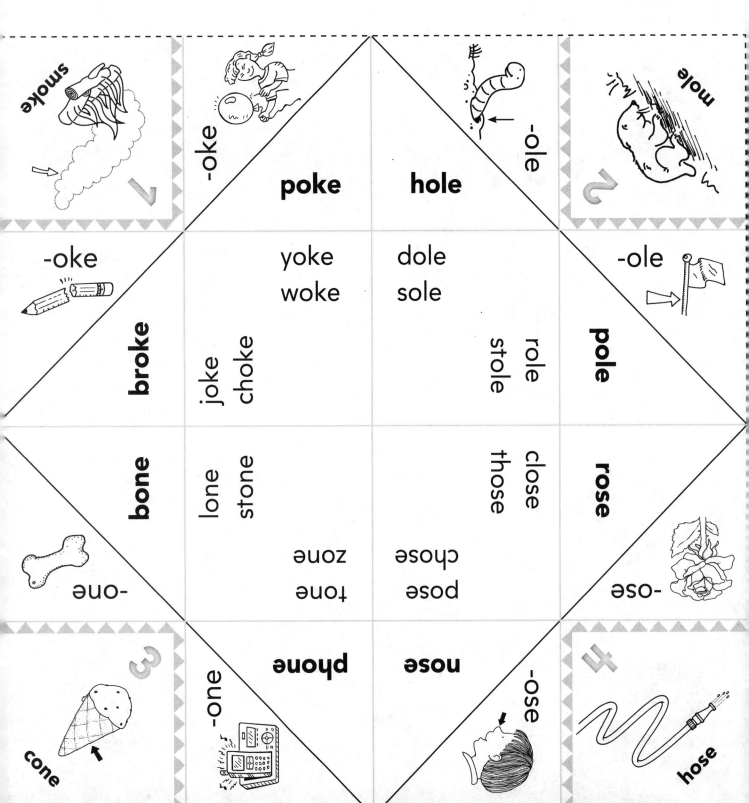

smoke

1

-oke

poke hole

-ole

2

mole

-oke

broke

yoke
woke

dole
sole

role
stole

pole

-ole

bone

joke choke

lone stone

close those

rose

-one

zone
tone

chose
pose

-ose

3

cone

-one

phone nose

-ose

4

hose

26 -oat, -oe, -old, -ow

Name the picture. Add the beginning sound to the word family ending.
Pick your favorite picture to start.

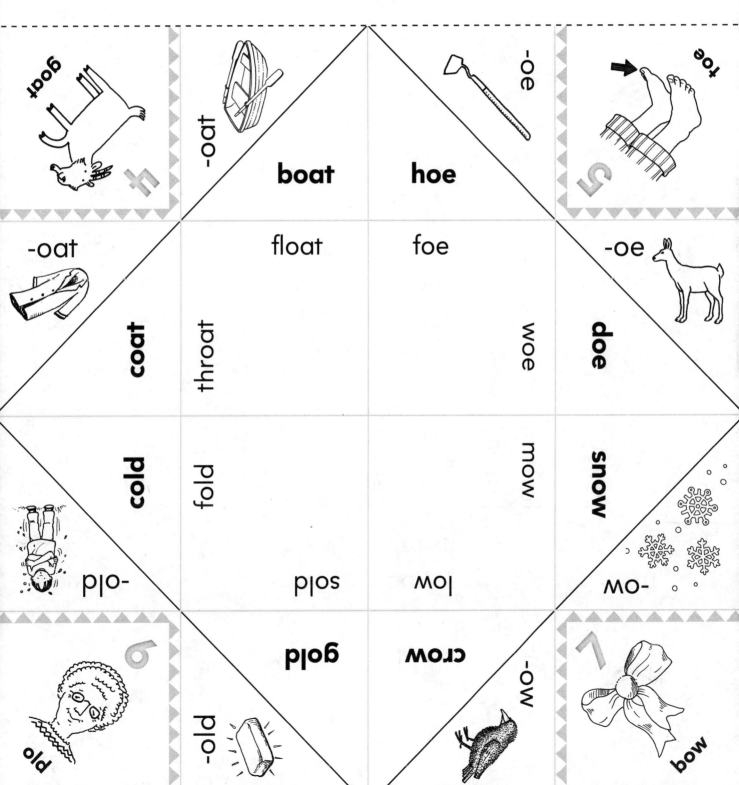

goat

-oat

-oe

toe

boat

hoe

4

5

-oat

float

foe

-oe

coat

throat

woe

doe

cold

fold

mow

snow

-old

sold

low

-ow

6

gold

crow

-ow

7

old

-old

bow

27 -all, -aw, -awn, -ew

Name the picture. Add the beginning sound to the word family ending.
Pick your favorite picture to start.

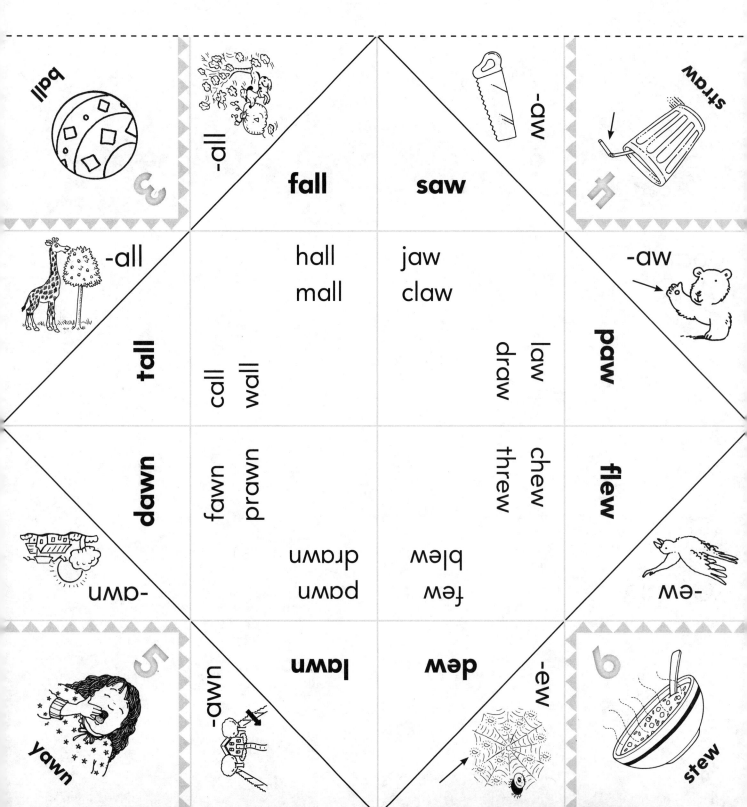

ball

3

-all

fall

saw

-aw

straw

4

-all

hall
mall

jaw
claw

-aw

tall

call wall

law
draw

paw

dawn

fawn prawn

chew
threw

flew

-awn

drawn
pawn

blew
few

-ew

5

yawn

-awn

lawn

dew

-ew

6

stew

28 -ook, -ool, -oom, -oot

Name the picture. Add the beginning sound to the word family ending.
Pick your favorite picture to start.

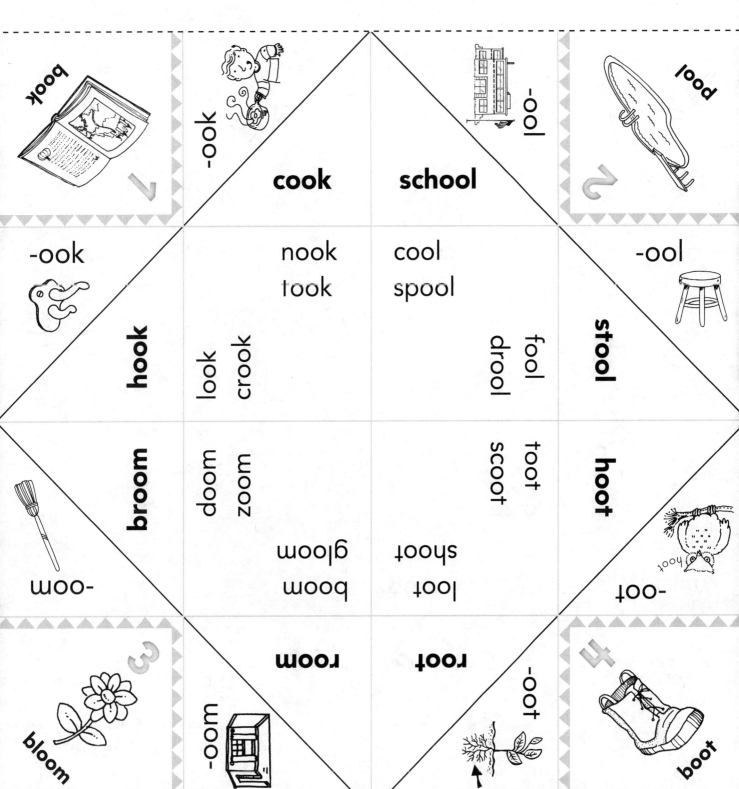

book

-ook

-ool

pool

cook   school

-ook

nook   cool

took   spool

-ool

stool

hook   look   crook   fool   drool

broom   doom   zoom   toot   scoot   hoot

-oom   gloom   shoot   hoot

-oot

boom   loot

room   root

-oom

-oot

bloom   boot

29 -oil, -ow, -own, -oy

Name the picture. Add the beginning sound to the word family ending.
Pick your favorite picture to start.

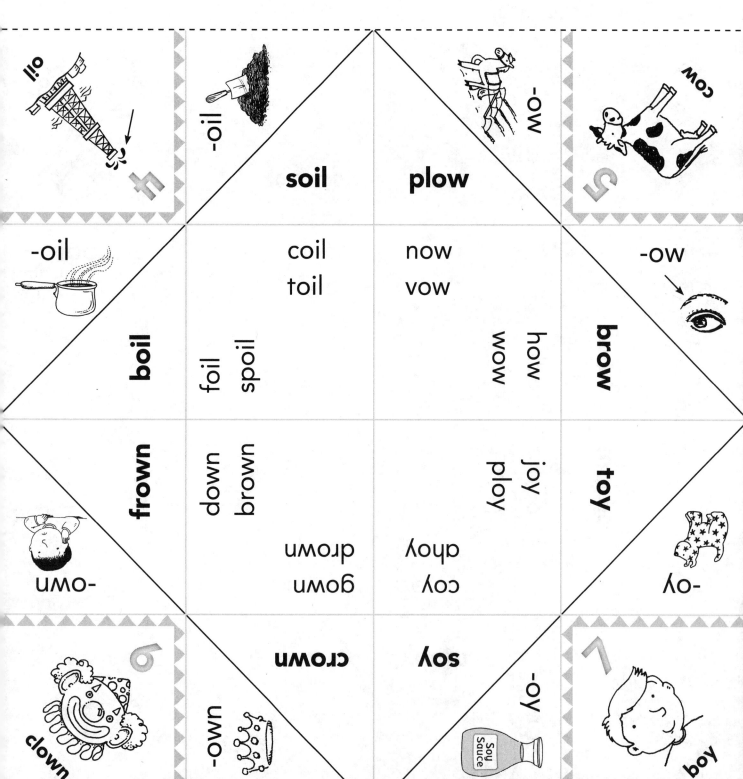

oil

-oil

4

soil

coil
toil

foil spoil

boil

-oil

-ow

5

cow

plow

now
vow

how
wow

-ow

brow

frown

down brown

drown
gown

ploy
joy

toy

-own

6

clown

-own

crown

soy

coy
ahoy

-oy

Soy Sauce

-oy

7

boy

30 -ouch, -ound, -ouse, -out

Name the picture. Add the beginning sound to the word family ending.
Pick your favorite picture to start.

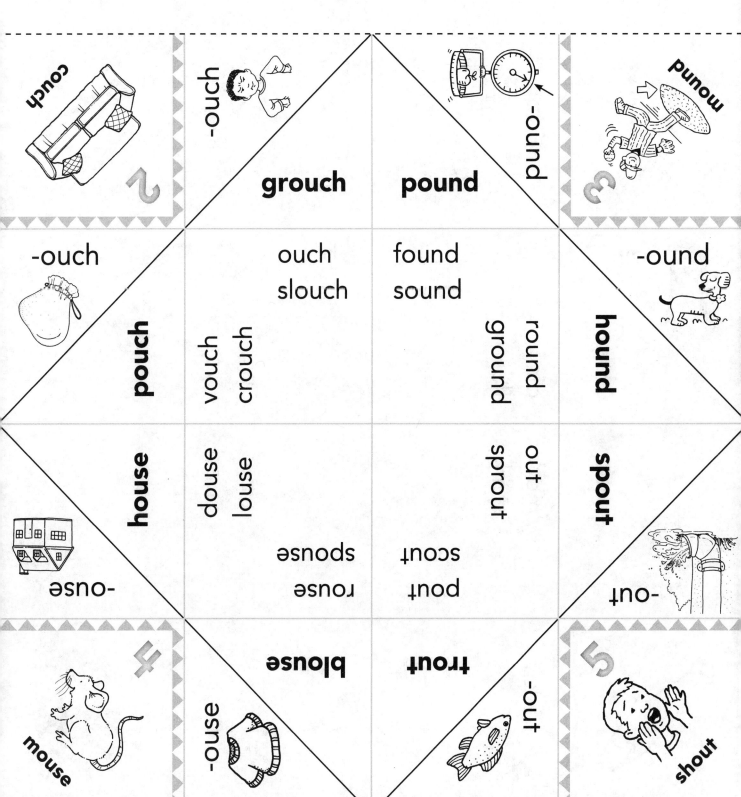

couch

2

-ouch

-ound

mound

3

grouch

pound

-ouch

ouch
slouch

found
sound

-ound

pouch

vouch | crouch

round
ground

hound

house

douse | louse

out
sprout

spout

spouse
rouse

scout
pout

-ouse

blouse

trout

-out

mouse

4

-ouse

5

-out

shout

31 -air, -ar, -ark, -art

Name the picture. Add the beginning sound to the word family ending.
Pick your favorite picture to start.

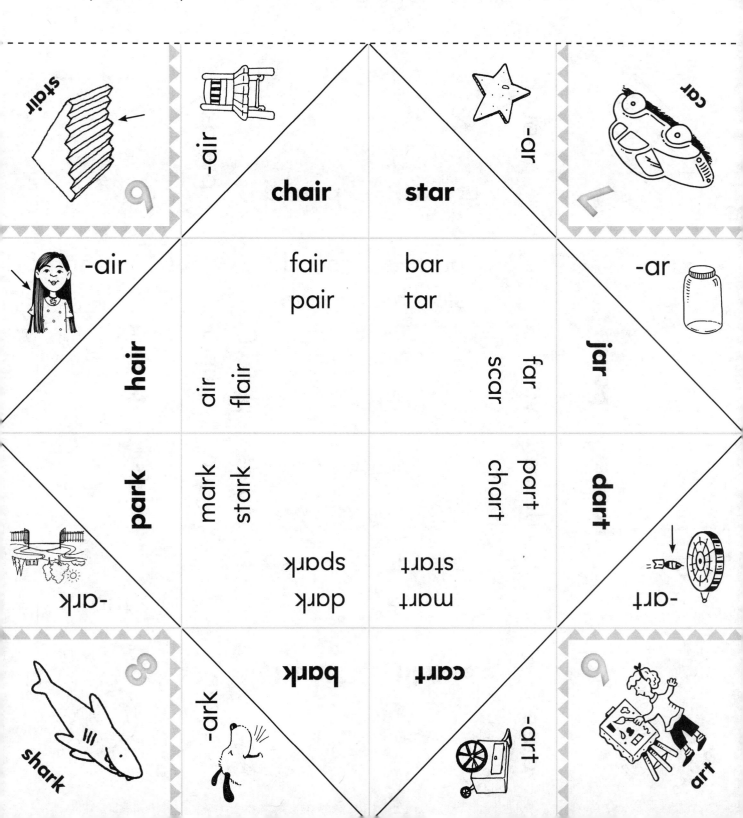

stair

-air

chair

-ar

star

car

-air

hair

fair
pair

bar
tar

jar

-ar

air
flair

far
scar

park

mark
stark

part
chart

dart

spark
dark

start
mart

-art

-ark

bark

cart

shark

-ark

-art

art

32 -ire, -irt, -ore, -orn

Name the picture. Add the beginning sound to the word family ending.
Pick your favorite picture to start.

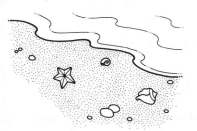

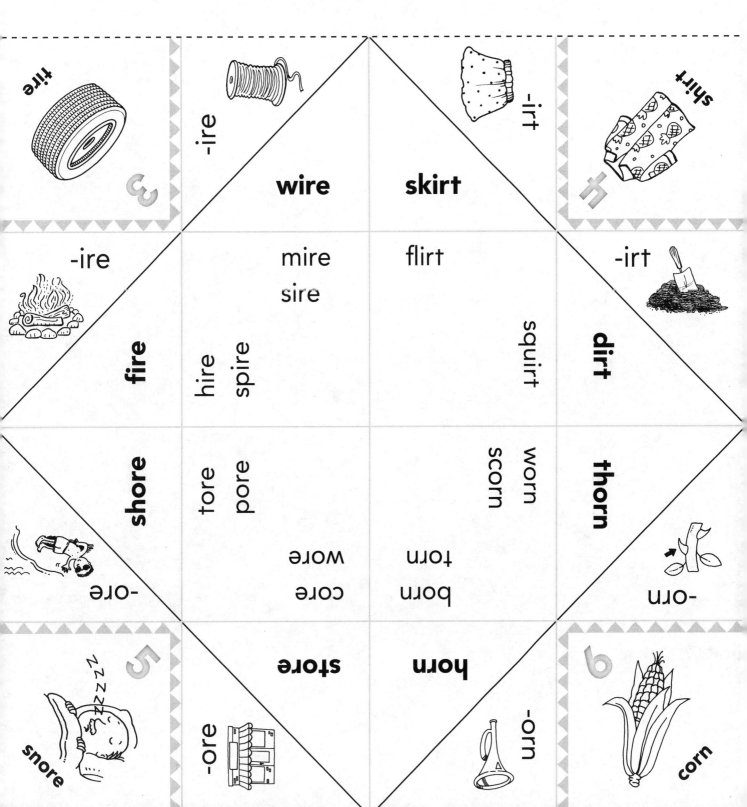

tire

-ire

3

-ire

fire

wire

mire
sire

hire   spire

shore

tore   pore

-ore

store

5

snore

-ore

-irt

skirt

flirt

squirt

worn
scorn

thorn

horn

-orn

shirt

4

-irt

dirt

-orn

6

corn

Fun Flap Template

Make your own fun flap!

1 Choose four word families. Draw (or glue) a picture for a different word family in each corner. Write a number from 2 to 9 in each circle.

2 Draw two more pictures for each word family in the spaces next to your first picture. Use the fun flaps in this book as a guide.

3 Write two words that belong to each word family on the set of lines near the center of your fun flap.

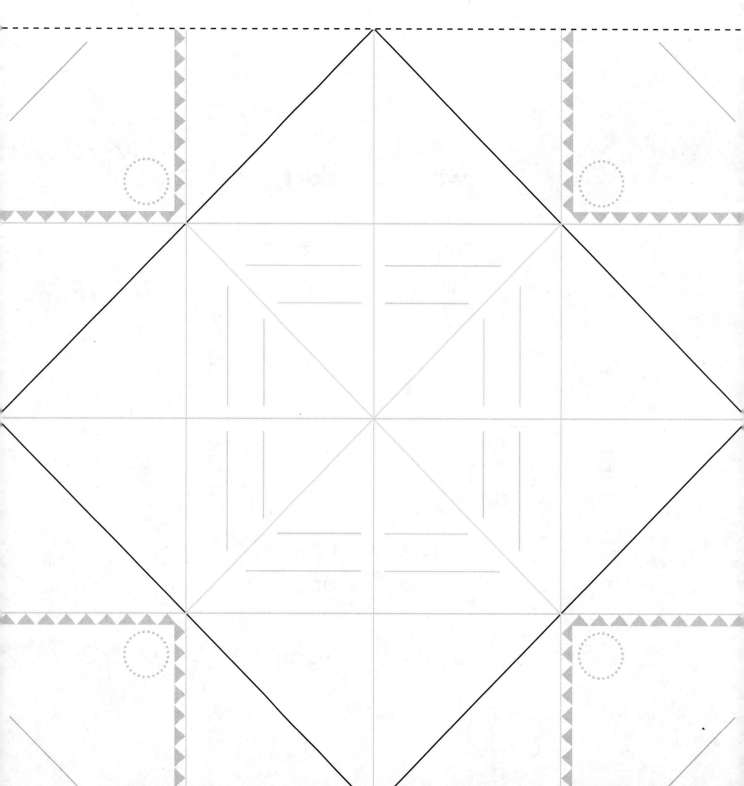